**Genre** Narrative N

MW00743567

 **Essential Question**
How are all living things connected?

# Saving San Francisco Bay
by Yvonne Morrin

# Chapter 1

# Something Must Be Done!

One day in 1960, Kay Kerr looked out her window. She looked across Berkeley Bay. Wind **rippled** the water. An osprey flew past. A heron hunted for food. Wildlife **flourished** in this part of San Francisco Bay.

Kerr and her friend Esther Gulick saw some bulldozers. The bulldozers were pushing soil and rocks into the water. Kerr and Gulick were not happy.

Many birds live in San Francisco Bay.

The bulldozers were filling in the Bay. They were making more land. San Francisco Bay is an **estuary**. An estuary is a place where freshwater mixes with salt water from the ocean. Many **species** of animals live there.

Kay Kerr was worried about the plans to fill in more of the Bay.

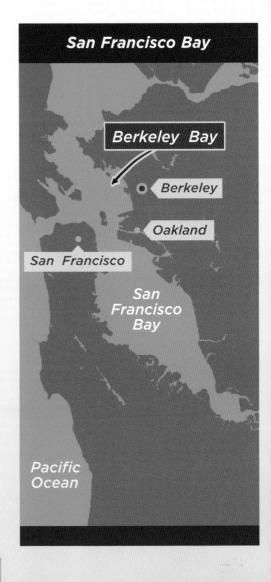

San Francisco Bay

Berkeley Bay

Berkeley

Oakland

San Francisco

San Francisco Bay

Pacific Ocean

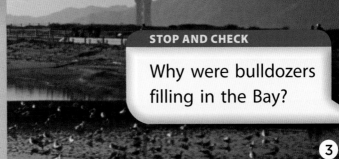

San Francisco Bay is a large estuary.

**STOP AND CHECK**

Why were bulldozers filling in the Bay?

3

A lot of San Francisco Bay was already filled in. Soon there might be no **shallow** areas left.

Kerr and Gulick wanted to protect the Bay. They knew that filling in the Bay would **destroy** the estuary. It would hurt the plants and animals. Some plants and animals might become **extinct**. Pollution was also a problem. Trash was polluting the Bay.

1849

1965

Berkeley Bay

2020 Prediction

San Francisco Bay has become smaller over time.

filled-in land

Kerr, Gulick, and their friend Sylvia McLaughlin talked to some groups. These groups helped take care of the environment. The groups were worried about the Bay, but they were too busy to help.

The women decided to save the Bay themselves.

Blue herons find their food in shallow water.

# Chapter 2

# Speaking Out

Kay Kerr and her friends started a group in 1961. They called it the Save San Francisco Bay Association (Save the Bay). The group sent out letters. The letters asked people to help protect the Bay. The women had a lot of **support**. Many people did not want the Bay filled in.

Esther Gulick, Sylvia McLaughlin, and Kay Kerr started Save the Bay.

In 1962, the Berkeley City Council said there was a plan to fill in more of Berkeley Bay. Berkeley Bay is part of San Francisco Bay. The plan would double the size of Berkeley City. The women's first goal was to stop this plan.

## WHY FILL IN THE BAY?

**Developers** and the Berkeley City Council wanted to make land for new buildings. The work would create new jobs and more money from taxes.

This oil refinery was built on the shores of San Francisco Bay.

The three friends needed more people to speak out about filling in the Bay. They sent more letters. The letters asked people to help save Berkeley Bay.

More people joined Save the Bay. The group sent letters asking the Berkeley City Council to stop its plan.

The women also talked to scientists. They asked them what would happen to Berkeley Bay if it were filled in.

The scientists said that filling in the Bay would cause an **imbalance** in the **ecosystem**. An ecosystem is a group of plants and animals that live together. Plants and animals in an ecosystem need each other for food. Some plants and animals would die if Berkeley Bay were filled in. Then there would be no food for other animals.

The women told these facts to the Berkeley City Council. The council decided to **limit** or control how much of Berkeley Bay could be filled in.

River otters eat fish from the shallow waters of the Bay.

**STOP AND CHECK**

Why did Berkeley City Council decide to limit the filling in of Berkeley Bay?

# Chapter 3

# The Fight Continues

The **fragile** ecosystem of Berkeley Bay was saved. The women then tried to save the rest of San Francisco Bay.

Kay Kerr met with a state senator. His name was Eugene McAteer. He started a group to look at all the plans for filling in the Bay.

The woman in this cartoon **represents**, or is a symbol for, San Francisco Bay. The man in the train wants to fill in the Bay. The other man is a law that will save the Bay.

Friday, June 18, 1965

CCCCAA

BAY FILL & S.F. SHORELINE RR.

McATEER PETRIS BILL

BAY

"Curses—foiled again!"

Save The Bay

Eugene McAteer
helped Save the Bay.

The senator's group talked to scientists. The scientists said that keeping the Bay safe would protect the environment.

Then Don Sherwood joined in. He was a radio announcer. He told people to write to the government about saving the Bay. The government listened. They passed a new law. The law said the state had to **approve**, or agree to, plans to fill in the Bay.

A new project was approved before the law passed in 1965. Developers wanted to **crumble** part of a mountain into soil. This soil would make more land in the Bay.

Kay Kerr (top), Sylvia McLaughlin (left), and Esther Gulick fought to protect San Francisco Bay.

## HUMAN DAMAGE

People in the 1960s did not know much about protecting the environment. They didn't know that people can damage the environment in the same way as a **drought** or an earthquake. Some people did not agree with Kay Kerr and her friends. They called them names.

Save the Bay wanted to stop the project. They sued the developers. They took them to court. The court case lasted for nine years. Finally an **agreement** was reached. The project was stopped. It was a win for Save the Bay!

**STOP AND CHECK**

How did Save the Bay stop the project?

13

Kay Kerr and Save the Bay members fought to take care of the environment. They showed that people can work together to make change.

The people in Save the Bay still work hard today to protect the environment. After all, people are part of the ecosystem, too.

Save the Bay is still cleaning up the Bay.

## Summarize

Why was it important to
save the Bay in *Saving San
Francisco Bay*? Use details to
summarize the selection.
Your graphic organizer may
help you.

| Main Idea |
| --- |
| Detail |
| Detail |
| Detail |

## Text Evidence

1. Reread Chapter 2. What is the main idea?
   Use details from the text in your answer.
   MAIN IDEA AND KEY DETAILS

2. Find the word *sued* on page 13. What does
   it mean? What clues help you figure it out?
   VOCABULARY

3. Write about what scientists said would
   happen if people filled in the Bay.
   Use details from page 9 in your answer.
   WRITE ABOUT READING

**Compare Texts**
Read about food webs and their
importance in an ecosystem.

# The
# Great Estuary Ecosystem

Many plants and animals live in the
estuary of San Francisco Bay. Clams and
mussels live in the mud. Fish, birds, and
mammals live in the water. Other birds
and mammals live on the shore.

These living things
depend on each other.
They are part of a
**food web**.

The California clapper
rail lives in the estuary.

Tiny plants grow in the shallow waters of the estuary. They are called phytoplankton. Seaweed grows there, too. These plants use energy from the sun to make food. They are called producers.

Mussels, shrimp, and small fish eat these plants. Otters eat the mussels, shrimp, and fish. The energy from the plants passes to the fish. The energy from the fish passes to the otters. Animals that eat plants or other animals are called consumers.

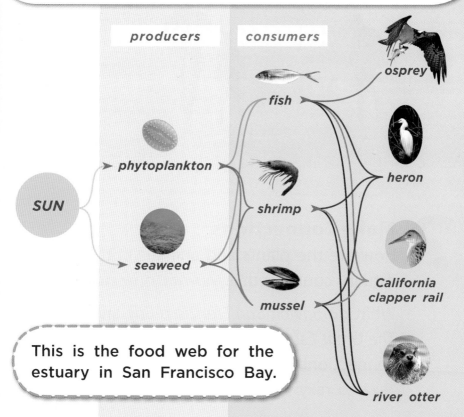

This is the food web for the estuary in San Francisco Bay.

People are part of food webs, too. People eat fish from San Francisco Bay. Animals and people will have less food if the ecosystem is damaged.

Children fish near San Francisco Bay.

## Make Connections

How are the plants and animals in the estuary connected? ESSENTIAL QUESTION

What do *Saving San Francisco Bay* and *The Great Estuary Ecosystem* show about connections between living things?

TEXT TO TEXT

# Glossary

**developers** *(di-VEL-uh-purz)* people or companies that build and sell buildings *(page 7)*

**estuary** *(ES-chuh-wer-ee)* an area where a river flows into an ocean *(page 3)*

**food web** *(fewd web)* a system where plants and animals feed off each other *(page 16)*

**species** *(SPEE-sheez)* a group of animals or plants that are similar *(page 3)*

# Index

# Focus on Science

**Purpose** To describe how living things are connected in a food web

## Procedure

**Step 1** Look at the food web diagram on page 17.

**Step 2** Think of another ecosystem with different plants and animals. These plants and animals need each other to live.

**Step 3** Draw a food web diagram for this ecosystem. Show how the plants and animals are connected.

**Step 4** Imagine that part of the web changes. What might happen?

**Step 5** Share your diagram with a partner.

**Conclusion** What have you learned about how living things need each other? A change in one part of a food web can change other parts. In what ways can a food web change?